NO EXCUSE
Travel Guide

A Blueprint for Making Your

Travel Dreams a Reality

by Philipp Gloeckl
co-Author: Kathy Tosolt

Publisher: Philipp Gloeckl

ISBN (Paperback): 978-1-7356453-0-8
ISBN (Hardcover): 978-1-7356453-1-5
ISBN (eBook): 978-1-7356453-2-2
ISBN (Audio Book): 978-1-7356453-3-9
Library of Congress Control Number: 2020916176

Some names and identifying details have been changed to protect the privacy of individuals. Any resemblance to actual persons, living or dead, or actual events is purely coincidental.

'Live life with no excuses, travel with no regret.'

- OSCAR WILDE

The

NO EXCUSE
Travel Guide

A Blueprint for Making Your

Travel Dreams a Reality

PREFACE

By the age of thirty I had visited over eighty countries and fulfilled my dream of visiting all the remaining Ancient & New Wonders of the World. These experiences have been some of the happiest and most rewarding times of my life - moments that have given me a great appreciation for the millions of people out there who long to see the world, but simply never get around to doing it.

For so many, the desire to travel goes unrealized due to a simple lack of execution. Uncertainty, inexperience or insufficient knowledge, lack of confidence and difficulty in kick-starting the motivation needed to take the plunge and do it prevent so many people from attaining their own fiercely desired dream to travel.

I've made it my personal mission to thoroughly analyze the most common reasons for travel success, and why travel plans often fail, to help those who long to make travel their reality. I've delved deep into my personal travel experiences and derived a sound set of practical, successfully used rules to inspire every person interested in traveling to stop making excuses and start exploring the world.

This book is a blueprint for creating a life of travel. It's the ideal resource to comfortably build your knowledge, help you overcome your travel obstacles, encourage you to chase your travel dreams, and push you to achieve your travel goals. It has been a pleasure and privilege to share my unique travel experiences and exceptional adventures with you.

My greatest wish is to encourage all types of explorers from all levels of society to expand their comfort zone and indulge in the world around us. Whether you're newly single, hoping to make the most of retirement with the love of your life, just starting out with your first weekend away, or eager to up your globetrotting game with the next big adventure, I hope to instill a sense of wonder in you, and open your physical and mental abilities to make a real, tangible difference in your life.

The beauty of the travel game is the endless sea of possibility and opportunity found in the everyday wonders that you discover for yourself when you do things your own way.

I want to thank everyone who has supported me and contributed towards making this book a reality. If it weren't for the unconditional love and wealth of personal experiences gained from the wonderful people I have met around the world, this book would never have been written.

I would like to thank Kathy Tosolt, my co-author and mentor, for her dedication and help making this travel book a success, my editor, Natalie Dent, as well as my dear friend and co-editor Tara Boinpally for challenging me to always see things from the reader's perspective. I also want to thank my family; my mother, Diana, my father, Hans and my sister, Anna, for their unwavering belief in me. I couldn't have imagined completing this travel book without their sincere emotional support.

I hope you enjoy reading my personalized travel rules and feel confident to successfully navigate the world and make your travel dreams reality[1].

Sincerely,

Philipp Gloeckl

---

[1] I would love to hear about your travels! Please feel free to connect with me on social media. My online travel persona is @TravelPeeGee.

PHOTO: That's Me! Sipping delicious coffee in the Sahara Desert, Morocco.

GUIDANCE
USING THE NO EXCUSE TRAVEL RULES

So you know you're keen to expand your travel activities and see more of the world. Before we dive in, let's take a moment to really think about what the word 'travel' means.

'Travel', according to the Cambridge dictionary, is 'to move or go from one place to another.' Depending on your perspective, 'travel' can mean enormously different things to vastly different people. For some people, travel is a work trip or a much-needed visit to see family in a far-off place. Some people view travel as a relaxing vacation on a tranquil beach in the sun, while others see it as an opportunity to explore their world in depth, unearthing new and exciting discoveries at every turn.

To me, **travel is a tool. It allows me to step out of my comfort zone and create unique experiences that boost my personal growth and understanding around me.**

Travel gives me a better perspective of my own life and shows me how my version of normal relates to other people's cultures. **What is ordinary to me is not always customary for others.** This distinction between traveling and simply taking a vacation is extremely important.

Throughout this book I will be referring to 'travel' as a means of stepping out of your comfort zone to engage with the world around you in a deep, meaningful way.

To guarantee your success as a traveling soul I highly recommend following all nine of my No Excuse Travel Rules, however these rules may be viewed and interpreted differently by each person. Understanding that there is always more than one way to accomplish your goals is essential.

The No Excuse Travel Rules have worked for me and many others who have also taken the leap, but they should not limit you from exploring and executing other travel tips and tricks.

These travel rules have been designed to help you attain your travel dreams, quell your excuses for not traveling, and leave you feeling free with no regrets. I'm here to share my knowledge from authentic travel experiences to show you how easy it is to put your ideas into action.

Travel can be a reality for anyone and everyone. Use this book as an inspirational tool to add to and personalize your existing travel knowledge. Be open-minded to every opportunity that comes your way and always be ready to take on the next big adventure however it presents itself.

The No Excuse Travel Rules are a blueprint for making your travel dreams your reality. As we move through each of the No Excuse Travel Rules, you'll find exercises to stretch your way of thinking and stimulate your creative thinking. Take the time to explore each idea in full, and share the things you learn with others.

The most important thing to remember is to have fun with it. Great travel, after all, creates great travelers!

PHOTO: Standing where Jesus Christ stood on the Mount of Olives, Jerusalem.

Rule 1
Start with a Travel Vision

'The biggest adventure you can take is to live the life of your dreams.'

- Oprah Winfrey

Everyone wants to be happy, and hopes to create great lasting memories. Using travel to find happiness allows us to peek into unknown spaces to enlarge our own perspective of the world.

Regardless of what inspires us to travel, we dream about beautiful places and picture ourselves having amazing experiences. We see ourselves exploring the Amazon jungle in South America, conquering Mount Everest, or witnessing cathedrals of ice crash beneath towering glaciers in Alaska. In our minds, we dance at Rio Carnival, savor Italian gelato in the shadow of Rome's ruined Colosseum, or imagine ourselves soaking up the enormous African sky on a Big 5 Safari in Kenya without a care in the world. As time goes by however, many of these wonderful travel goals peter out, so in the end, nothing gets accomplished. Our fleeting travel thoughts and detailed daydreams fail to take shape as authentic, well-conceived, achievable travel visions. Writing a clear travel vision requires digging deep inside yourself to interrogate one of life's most important questions:

*"When I reach the end of this life,
will I regret not having seen more?"*

The key is to ask yourself, "What do I need to accomplish with my travels over my lifetime to ensure I have no regrets?" This idea has always been the cornerstone for creating the kind of travel vision that has really locked-in and secured my lifetime travel goals. Why? Because one day you won't be able to go back and change it.

Having a personal travel wish list sets you up with measurable, obtainable travel goals that can easily be reached by anyone who sets their heart to doing it. It's not enough to dream of travel in a light, airy way. Your travel dreams should be specific, tailored to your unique interests and filled with all the juicy details that will intrigue and delight your curiosity, encouraging you to reach out and grab what lies beyond your comfort zone.

Photo: A gorgeous summer evening in the Swiss Alps, Switzerland.

Think about your personal travel vision. **What inspires you, challenges your ideals and leaves you feeling excited?** Follow your instinct. The first answer is usually a beautiful place to start.

If I could go anywhere, where would it be?

If I could travel with anyone, who would it be?

What excites me the most about traveling?

What do I hope to learn by stepping out of my comfort zone?

Travel visions can, do, and should alter over time. Like all dreams, the ideas you had when you were a young child are likely to be quite different from your current aspirations as an adult. But, this does not mean your childhood dreams don't carry value into your adult life. Creating a successful travel vision is an ongoing process that requires you to constantly question and evaluate your personal travel goals as your travels progress.

When you travel more frequently, your travel vision will develop with you, leading you to deeper, more immersive experiences within the context of your own travel dreams. Your main travel goal should be to have a lifetime of no regrets, while constantly adjusting your travel vision to allow new opportunities to present themselves within your own travel story.

Once you've created a clear vision of your travel ideas, it is essential to remember that your travel dream is your own vision for your own personal journey. Feel confident about what you plan to achieve, and don't let others encourage you to question YOUR travel vision or force you to rethink it. As crazy as it sounds, don't be afraid to name it. Have the courage to speak up and talk about it. If needed, shout it out and make it your own. Once you have the courage to believe in yourself and your personally defined travel vision, you will have the foundation in place to successfully turn your ideas into real, tangible actions.

I've always had big goals and outrageous travel dreams. I wanted to travel the world on my own terms, to live as a globetrotter in a way that most people thought was impossible. People laughed at me, told me I was crazy, but I knew I needed to believe it for myself before any of my dreams could take shape.

It was the doubt shown by others that made me realize my travel goals were finally big enough to properly inspire me, so I took the leap and I've never looked back. I use the doubts of others to my advantage, so when people tell me the life I want can't be obtained, I feel motivated and challenged to prove them wrong.

When I sat down to write my own travel vision, I wrote it as though everything had already been achieved. Rather than viewing my dreams as separate to my life, I treated my travel goals as real stories that were already part of my own personal experience.

This was my very first travel vision, exactly as written a long time before I set off on my life's greatest travel adventure:

✈ I've explored all the remaining Ancient and New Wonders of the World.

✈ I've traveled to every country in the world.

✈ I've lived in different countries, as part of a foreign society, as well as a smaller community.

✈ I've explored Central and South America by myself.

✈ I've fished on all the Great Lakes of Michigan.

✈ I've shared my adventures with family and friends, and written a travel book to inspire other people all around the world to travel.

✈ I've created enough streams of income and developed a strategy of financial security that will allow me to freely travel the world for the rest of my life.

Achieving these massive travel goals has expanded them into new goals. These dreams did not magically happen overnight, nor were they achieved by hoping they might fall into place on their own someday. It took a tremendous amount of stamina and discipline to turn the life I had into the life I have now, but this has been worth every drop of effort.

Each day, morning and evening, I write down my goals as well as my achievements. Every goal is written down quickly, but thoughtfully. By doing this, I continuously remind myself of my unclouded vision and focus, especially when things look like they're stacked against me or failure seems inevitable. Every travel goal I have ever set for myself has started with my personally defined travel vision. It is my on-going drive and "never stop exploring" travel mentality that enables me to continue creating new travel visions every day.

Create a travel vision that genuinely excites you. Use your imagination and interests to shape your own travel desires and don't allow yourself to feel trapped by social expectations. Always remember, **the ones who are trying to talk you out of your dreams are usually the ones who have already given up on theirs.**

Focus on your own story, write your own travel vision and never lose sight of the dreams you build within the space of your own imagination.

Photo (Top): Riding the Pyramids of Giza, Egypt.
Photo (Bottom): Ice fishing on the Great Lakes of Michigan.

Rule 2

Commit to Becoming a Traveler

'It doesn't matter where you are. You are nowhere compared to where you can go.'

- Bob Proctor

I didn't achieve all my personal travel wishes in one sitting. They were accomplished little by little, each driven by one major principle: **to make a conscious decision to be a world traveler.** This is a daily mentality that I have standardized for myself. I want and choose to travel, every day, which enables me to always take the next step and action toward my travel vision.

I've always wanted to travel the world on my own terms, and I've been fortunate to visit over eighty countries, but the most exciting part of all is that I always know the best is yet to come. Each experience has expanded my understanding of myself and the world around me. Every journey has reinforced my commitment to travel, always following through with my plans regardless of any hardships and personal obstacles that may come my way. It hasn't always been easy, but it has always been worth it.

It's not surprising so many people can easily access their explorer's imagination and pepper their travel dreams with ambitious plans for adventures. Aspiring globetrotters excitedly follow rule number one, 'Start with a Travel Vision,' and come up with sensational dreams filled with wild journeys and life-changing experiences. They start sharing their travel minds with others and find new ways to fulfill their deepest hopes, then simply never leave the ground, and never really know why they didn't get around to doing it.

What these people lack is relentless commitment to becoming a traveler. Simply put, they lose steam as soon as travel requires effort. **To become a traveler, it is necessary to go all out to make sure that it actually happens. Commit first and figure the rest out later.** In other words, get started before you feel ready, so that when the time comes to start traveling, there are no excuses holding you back or restricting you to your comfort zone.

This approach may make you feel challenged or uncomfortable at times, but this is how you will know you are finally moving in the right direction. You should, and will, outgrow your comfort zone. Embrace this process - it's an empowering feeling!

Once you have committed to travel, the thought of hesitation, rejection or retreat all lose the power to stop you from executing your plans. Those without a real travel commitment approach a critical point of weakness and start fooling themselves into believing things are not working out. Non-committed travelers question themselves and weigh the choice to either go for it or take the easier route and opt out. Many opt out, never fulfilling their dreams or allowing themselves to have the wonderful life they deserve.

If your travel vision is aligned with your heart's desire to travel, and you are sincerely committed to fulfilling your true travel potential, you won't doubt yourself, and you won't make soft excuses. Instead, you'll channel the time you would otherwise have spent questioning yourself into investing in your travel planning and pursuing your dreams wholeheartedly. **One of the most valuable pieces of advice I have ever received is to never explain myself. The results speak for themselves.**

Regardless of any hardships or challenges I've faced, I continue to follow through with my plans because of my ongoing personal commitment to living a life of travel.

Your biggest fans in life seldom need an explanation, they simply understand, and the naysayers won't buy into your explanations no matter how hard you try to explain yourself, so don't waste your time with either. As with all things in life, success demands that you use your time and energy wisely to navigate yourself towards achieving your goals. Remember, this is a one-way street! Focus your goals in one direction only, heading straight and forward.

You may start to notice that many travel-dreamers justify their lack of travel with similar excuses. Phrases such as "there is too much at stake" or "have you heard about the crime rate over there?" and "I can't really afford to travel at the moment" are some of the most popular reasons why travel is thought to not be possible. The pool of excuses runs deep, and those who are looking to find one will always come up with something to stop themselves from choosing a life of travel.

Successfully committing to removing your excuses, and ignoring any excuses imposed on you by others, requires that you continuously ask yourself one particularly important question:

"How IS it possible for me to travel the world?"

What can YOU do to make your travel possible? Ask yourself this question as often as possible and pay attention to how your answers change over time.

EXERCISE

Write down 5 of your favorite excuses that have stopped you from traveling:

1.

2.

3.

4.

5.

Think about some of the excuses you have made to avoid committing to your travel plans, then use the space below to ask yourself; *"What can I do now to remove these obstacles and make my travel possible?"*

When I started to genuinely take responsibility for my life, I learned how to feel in control of my travel dreams. Committing to something is not always easy. It requires willingness, discipline and initiative to fight against your inner villains and external roadblocks. Once you do this, however, it always pays off and rewards your efforts with everything you can imagine for yourself and more.

Of all the reasons people find to not travel, **a perceived lack of money is the number one obstacle to resolve**. This is often the toughest challenge faced by those hoping to travel, because the reality of travel is that it does cost some money. The good news is, it's a relatively easy goal to accomplish as long as you are willing to create a strategy to strengthen your personal travel fund.

Travel doesn't need to be expensive, but it is essential to understand your own financial situation and how it relates to your travel vision.

We all come from various levels of society and some are more financially prosperous than others, but money - or a lack thereof - shouldn't hold you back. Finding the money needed starts with a strategy based on two simple questions: *"What is my financial starting point"* and *"How much money do I need to be able to do the things I want to do?"*

Once you fully understand your personal financial situation and know what you need to save to be able to make your goals a reality, you can make the changes necessary to reallocate your money towards your travel plans. Finding the money to travel has a clear roadmap with measurable goals.

STEP 1: ASSESS YOUR CURRENT FINANCIAL SITUATION

Surprisingly, travel doesn't cost much but there are some minimum requirements needed to get started. Usually, the biggest expense is the plane ticket. Once that's accounted for, visiting a different place need not be any more expensive than staying at home, and sometimes it can work out cheaper than staying at home, especially in lower-cost destinations such as Vietnam and Thailand. *Your ability to understand and track your finances will determine your level of travel success.* Having money available for travel is a matter of using the money you do have more efficiently. Learning to captain your financial ship gives you better control over it and opens more doors as a result.

Analyze your current financial resources to determine your overall available budget for travel. While some expenses are fixed and may need to take priority, other expenses can easily be rearranged and repurposed in line with your commitment to fulfilling your travel vision.

STEP 2: RE-EVALUATE YOUR CURRENT PRIORITIES WITH TRAVEL IN MIND

Ask yourself, *"Do I really not have the money, or do I just spend my money on other things?"*

In short, if you can afford to buy a coffee every morning you can afford to travel, you just need to get your priorities straight. Looking at it another way, a plane ticket to just about anywhere in the world costs less than the latest smartphone.

Would making a coffee at home for your daily commute, rather than buying one at the station, make coffee taste all the sweeter when you're drinking authentic Italian coffee on the shores of the Amalfi Coast in Italy? Would having a cheaper phone be just as useful to you on your dream trip to Asia as the latest phone release would be photographing your kale smoothie at home?

Photo: Sipping ice-cold beer on the beach in the Bahamas.

Saving for travel does mean foregoing some of the creature comforts that may seem like a priority to you now, but with time you'll find it's relatively easy to live without most things if you have the right mindset. Once you are committed to saving for travel, spending money on upgrading technology and other frivolous luxuries begins to seem wasteful and counterproductive towards your bigger financial goals.

It's easy to splurge, and harder to save. This is because spending money is a way of soothing ourselves with treats. Saving takes discipline, but if you start with small steps and develop a focused mindset to spend your money more wisely on your top priorities, you will set yourself up for a lifetime of sound financial decision-making, with a healthy budgeting mentality.

Hint: Set up a separate bank account for your travel fund. Pay your traveling self with a monthly direct debit, always treating yourself as your highest financial priority. Paying yourself **first** makes active saving a habit, removes the money you are saving from your subconscious spending pot and may also earn you some extra interest in the right bank account.

Photo: Seeing the blood red sun rise across the Australian Outback.

'Pay the price now so you can pay any price in the future.'
- GRANT CARDONE

Whether you're traveling on a shoestring or visiting top-spend destinations, the budget needed for your travel is less important than your desire to travel and your commitment to traveling. In other words, find a travel budget that works for you and tailor your travel vision to suit what you can comfortably afford, rather than aiming for something that's out of your reach and struggling to find the money for it.

This approach is more effective than creating overly expensive travel plans that are unrealistic for you, and gives you easy to reach budgeting goals that can and will make your travel dreams come true. It doesn't matter if your budget is big or small, if it's comfortable for you.

STEP 3: INCREASE YOUR INCOME WITH A BETTER JOB, OR FIND A SIDE HUSTLE

Sometimes improving your financial situation to afford travel means switching to a higher-paying job or finding a successful side hustle. This is easier than it seems, and most people can harvest their skills to earn extra money using their existing resources. You may like to run errands for the elderly, sell some of your art, start an ecommerce business, or take a course to move up the career ladder.

The possibilities are endless, and most of today's work can be done online while you are traveling. If you commit yourself to channeling a second source of income, you will always have a passive way to fund your travel plans.

My great friend and personal hero, Pravin, is a splendid example of how anyone can improve their financial situation with commitment and focus. Pravin was born and raised in poverty on a remote farm in India. At the time of writing this book it was normal for a farmer in India to earn as little as $3 per day, so Pravin's outlook was poor from the start. Few people in his village ever moved beyond the confines of poverty, so it was assumed that Pravin should take up the life of a farmer as soon as he was old enough to start working.

Pravin walked five miles to and from elementary school every day, just to attend a higher quality school than the one in his village. He hoped he might one day be able to lift himself into a richer life if he gained a stronger education. Throughout his childhood, Pravin's father challenged and rewarded him to become a better version of himself every day, a task Pravin took very seriously. Years later, all his hard work paid off with a role as a financial analyst in the city of Pune, far away from his life on the farm.

Soon after starting his new job, Pravin was relocated to work in the United States where he fulfilled his lifelong dream of seeing beyond the shores of India and the remote farm he grew up on.

His dedication and commitment to improving his skills enabled him to earn a high salary and live a comfortable life. Increasing his income afforded Pravin the luxury of also being able to travel on his own terms. He has now experienced much of the world due to his sheer determination to create a better financial situation for himself rather than just accepting the life of poverty he was born into.

Pravin once told me that aside from meeting his wife, moving to America was the best thing that ever happened to him. Without his deep-seated hunger to develop and expand himself, Pravin may never have left his farm in India. His commitment to becoming an explorer profoundly changed his life.

Now it's your turn to make a commitment to yourself to chase the life you know you deserve. Allow yourself to have it with no excuses.

Photo: Admiring Horseshoe Bend at the Grand Canyon.

Rule 3

Be Grateful, Think Positively

'To live is the rarest thing in the world. Most people just exist.'

- Oscar Wilde

Have you ever stopped to consider how even the slightest change in the circumstances surrounding your birth may have created an entirely different person?

This life you have been given is completely yours, and you are free to do whatever it is that makes you happy. To me, this creates an enormous sense of gratitude for the life I have, which is why I have made the decision to spend my life exploring my world. I use my body every possible way that I can to extract all of the goodness out of everything my life can be.

I believe the key to a successful existence is to be genuinely happy, and to spread nothing but **love, optimism, gratitude and positive thinking in every way imaginable.** It is only when we open our hearts to others and live with a sense of mindfulness for everything around us that we are truly liberated as people and travelers.

I've noticed, during thousands of interactions with culturally diverse people from some remarkably different parts of the world, a high percentage of people automatically default to having a negative attitude rather than a positive perspective.

Instead of truly valuing, appreciating, and understanding life as a genuine gift with plenty of messy details to celebrate, many people like to dwell on the shortcomings, often focusing on all the things they should or shouldn't have done. Everybody wants to win the lottery, but what few people realize is that life itself, with the simple joys that make us human, is the biggest lottery jackpot of all. We've all won just by being here.

Once you appreciate the power of harnessing joy, you'll develop a healthy perspective with a positive undertone.

Photo: Soaring without a care in the world in Cape Town, South Africa.

Having the strength to stop taking things for granted, and to stop complaining, lifts the lid on all the things that hold you back and allows you to live and express yourself to your fullest potential. Sure, life isn't always fair, and chances are you'll have your share of tough times - we all do. Some have it much harder than others, but always remember that problems are no more than a series of interconnected challenges and opportunities to be taken by anyone who is brave enough to see them as a positive force. Embrace the challenges, and the opportunities will present themselves.

When we waste time dwelling on negative experiences, rather than just accepting the storms we face, we move away from a place of gratitude and create endless excuses to stop ourselves living the life we genuinely deserve. Negative thinking never gets anyone far in life.

Today's times allow us to connect and travel at levels never seen before. Globalization, advanced technology and our insatiable desire for knowledge is driving an age of travel that's accessible to anyone with ambition to learn and a willingness to try new things. We're now able to work and live just about anywhere in the world with nothing more than a laptop and a decent internet connection. This makes the ability to travel an everyday reality that's yours to enjoy however you wish!

Staying positive is essential; it holds the key to living a happy life. By its very nature, positive thinking can only enhance. It is a choice you can make for yourself at any moment, on any given day. The power of positive thinking has a remarkable ability to renew and feed off its own energy, eventually becoming a default way of thinking that primes you for success in every aspect of life.

Acknowledging the magic of positive thinking has genuinely changed my life for the better, and it can do the same for you if you are willing to embrace life's simplest pleasures and find the joy in every moment.

'Whether you think you can, or you think you can't - you're right.'
- HENRY FORD

It's widely accepted that the average person has between 12,000 and 60,000 thoughts per day, of which close to 80% are negative. Much like staying positive, when we think in negative tones we become negative thinkers, putting up barriers for ourselves before we've even begun. Negativity saps our energy, drains the brain and sends our emotions reeling, which can leave us feeling stressed, demotivated and unable to find the good in any situation.

This cycle of negativity so often prevents people from chasing their travel dreams, which is why it's so important to stay positive. Seek authentic happiness and always strive to be content with your life, even when things seem tough. This sets you up for greatness with the confidence to achieve anything you set your mind to.

Evidence suggests we are the combined average of the six people we spend the most time with. This doesn't mean you should question your entire network, but you should be aware of who is in your life and how they influence you. Surround yourself with people who contribute towards your success. Be in tune with the people who support you when it matters most. Be mindful too of those you feel are supportive of you, as these people are often a direct reflection of the things you value most in your own life.

Photo: Reflecting joy at Salar de Uyuni, Bolivia.

Think about the people in your life and how they make you feel. Who elevates your mood with their positivity and joy?

Who brings you down, drains your mood or makes you feel not good enough?

You may just find that you are the most negative person you know! **How could implementing positive thinking make a difference to others in your life?**

Not only do your surroundings affect your well-being, but YOU TOO can affect your surroundings. How much love and positivity can you bring to your neighborhood or local community? **If you really think about it, how much could you contribute to the world around you if you set your mind to it?**

There are no limits, and you may already be having a significant impact on those around you. Your positive message can and will be absorbed, reproduced, multiplied and returned to you tenfold if you open your heart to all the good things that having a positive attitude can do for you. Now, think about this from a global perspective and imagine how deeply the attitudes of those who travel affect the world.

Positivity creates more positivity with change for good, which has a ripple effect on those we encounter when we travel with a happy mindset. Traveling with optimism and a healthy dose of positive energy not only provides you with a solid base to pursue your happy adventures, but harnesses your international network to spread your global understanding and cultural awareness to others around the world, with lasting benefits that are felt by everyone you meet on your personal journey.

Think about your social network and how the people in your life affect your positive attitude, then ask yourself:

✈ Who am I spending the most time with?

✈ Who supports me in my dream to travel?

✈ Who in my life helps me accomplish the goals I set for myself?

✈ How does social media and the online content I absorb affect my attitude?

✈ What keeps me feeling inspired to travel?

Embracing positive thinking is a lesson I learned the hard way during the initial stages of my travels. I neglected the importance of positive thinking and paid for it dearly in wasted time and lost enjoyment. **My negative attitude and feelings of entitlement led to anger and frustration when things didn't go my way, which left me feeling disconnected and constantly challenged by my travel mishaps.** I now consider positive thinking to be paramount to every successful travel experience.

Having a different attitude has meant travel is now a richly rewarding experience that affects me positively in ways I could never have imagined. My previously negative approach developed my sense of regret for missed opportunities, all of which could have been avoided had I only looked at things differently.

I had, for example, planned a trip to Rio Carnival in Brazil with a bunch of my buddies, but when they all dropped out my insecurities about traveling alone meant I decided not to go, for no valid reason. I should have gone to Rio, and I know now that I would have had fun and made new friends.

When I first moved to Los Angeles, I made some poor financial choices in Las Vegas. I lost some money, which not only restricted my future travel plans but also frustrated me to the point where I decided to stop traveling. This was based on my incorrect belief that everything related to travel was suddenly beyond my means. Instead of giving up entirely, I should have adjusted my travel vision to enjoy smaller, more budget-friendly experiences that would still allow me to build up my travel fund over time. This would have helped me reach my financial goals without missing out on any of the less expensive travel opportunities I often enjoy today.

Looking back now, I can see that my negative attitude manifests itself in specific, measurable ways:

✈ I expected too much of others without realizing my travel plans are always my own responsibility.

→ I was closed-minded when it came to my perceived social rules, so I found it challenging to adjust my relatively fixed German belief that everything should be orderly, defined and structured.

→ My travel was all about me, with little genuine interest in learning from other people or experiencing other points of view.

→ Whenever I felt stressed or overwhelmed, I blamed others, believing they were the reason for all the challenges I was facing within my own experiences.

→ My lack of perspective meant I was unwilling to open myself up to the happiness travel brings, and instead always focused on problems rather than opportunities.

The first thing I did to rectify my attitude was to observe the circle of people I was spending the most time with. I assessed how they were influencing me, realized who was holding me back and stopped hanging out with people who had a negative impact on my life. I quietly moved away from all those who restricted my goals or made me feel insecure.

It may sound harsh to prune relationships like this, but **we are, after all, the product of the company we keep. Real change takes bold decisions.** Surround yourself with like-minded, inspiring people who challenge you to be your best version of yourself every day. Once I had sorted out my positive attitude, I discovered how easy it is to open doors into wonderful spaces with unplanned opportunities. I learned how to solve problems on my feet and discovered the value of embracing challenges to enhance my travels, rather than hinder them.

The first challenge arrived when I was traveling in the Galapagos Islands and decided to try my novice hand at expert scuba diving. We were at Gordon Rocks, where sea currents regularly reach dangerously strong levels, and my limited diving experience meant I was significantly under-prepared for the dive. When a hammerhead shark brushed past me 90ft under the surface of the ocean I drained my oxygen tank in one terrified gulp!

My new attitude meant I had joined the dive group alone but had luckily also made several new friends in the group. Seeing my widening eyes, a fellow diver kindly shared some of his own emergency oxygen with me and I managed to avoid a quiet death on the ocean floor. Later, we enjoyed a thank-you beer in the local bar feeling completely exhilarated, profoundly bonded by our near-death experience with the shark.

On self-reflection, my positive attitude now looks like this:

- ✈ Always be kind. Positivity always wins.

- ✈ Be friendly and engaging. Always aim to put a smile on other people's faces.

✈ Embrace humility around other people.

✈ Appreciate other people's heritage, culture, history, religion and language even if it seems outrageous or different from anything you know.

✈ Provide help and support to others without any expectation of something in return.

✈ Be grateful for everything, and make the most of every experience, good or bad.

✈ Don't waste time or energy dwelling on the negative.

✈ Lower expectations. That way there's always room for surprise.

This attitude defines who I am today and how I live my travel life. Get your positive mindset right and don't be afraid to play with it - you'll always be rewarded!

Photo (Top): Early morning sunrise in the Amazon Jungle, Bolivia.

Photo (Bottom): Exploring the quaint streets of Havana, Cuba.

Rule 4
Love it … Or Change it

'Never complain about something you're not willing to change.'
- Inky Johnson

Every day we encounter inconvenient situations, some of which may require life-changing decisions. When we fail to make decisions for ourselves, other people can make our decisions for us with or without our own input. Letting others make decisions for you gives other people control over the things that affect your life, which is never ideal when it comes to finding happiness and following your own dreams on your own terms.

In the previous chapter we explored the power of positive thinking and the impact it can have on your life. Positive thinking leads to an abundance of travel adventures. In the same way that positive thinking opens new opportunities, so does having an action-orientated attitude when making decisions.

Action mobilizes your positive thoughts into real, tangible experiences. For example, you may not enjoy your job much. You might not want to work for your employer, but you understand that having your job is necessary to pay for your comfortable lifestyle. You may feel as though your boss or your work tasks create the unhappiness in your job, but what you should really be asking yourself is,

"What can I DO to improve this situation for myself?"

Ultimately, the only person responsible for your life and the experiences you create for yourself is you. Having a positive, action-orientated attitude gives you tools to take control. You could ask for a meeting to discuss your work environment. You could improve your own communication skills by attending a seminar to learn how to work with difficult people and how to manage workplace conflict. You could also change your department, get a new job, or switch professions entirely to create a completely different path for yourself that's better aligned to what you would like to do. This may sound challenging, but it is all very possible with the right approach. It starts with a firm decision to make the changes needed to resolve your unfavorable situation, then taking action with a positive, can-do attitude.

What you simply can't do – assuming you want to improve your personal situation – is complain about your job, do nothing about it to change your situation, and expect it to improve on its own. Inaction is a manifestation of negative thinking, so your decision to do nothing is a firm decision not to take control over your own experience, and your own life.

Learn to love your situation or change it to something you are happier with. It's your responsibility, and your responsibility alone, to create a life you love.

Linking your positive thinking to decisive action dictates that you will no longer allow yourself to become trapped in toxic situations that consume your precious time and energy. Being the only person in charge of your own life's outcomes means you must act intentionally, with personal integrity.

Once you fully embrace a 'love it or change it' attitude you will be empowered to take control over your life. The same principle applies to fulfilling your travel plans. If you feel stagnant, bored with life and wish to travel more, then the only solution is to make an active decision to travel, and actually do it!

My own travels began with a shift in my attitude about traveling alone.

We were slowly but steadily approaching the end of our study semester in San Diego when I met my friend, Mike, for a drink at a lively bar in Pacific Beach. We exchanged our different thoughts and views on travel, and Mike enthusiastically told me story after story about his exciting life that was always filled with travel. As I listened to his crazy adventures, completely captivated by the things he had done, it struck me that he had always traveled by himself! Until then I had never traveled alone, and felt traveling alone was something I just couldn't really see myself being comfortable with. I had a plethora of reasons holding me back. Fear of loneliness, boredom, concerns for my personal safety and general inexperience meant I had always found someone to travel with or chosen the easier route of simply staying at home. Mike was amazed by this.

"Do you know how much you are missing out on in life while waiting around for other people?!"

Mike was right, of course, and this resonated deep within me. I was missing out on fully living my life because I was always waiting for my circumstances to be perfect. The myth of the so-called *'perfect moment'* does not exist. Mike's attitude about traveling alone had a fundamental impact on my understanding of travel.

It took me years to fully understand what this meant, but eventually it sunk in and I realized the only way to create true happiness is to genuinely love what you have, and if you don't love it, to change it!

Photo: Travelling alone in Cape Town, South Africa.

Time is an extremely precious resource that is finite and measurable, so I made a conscious decision to live with no regrets and to allow myself no excuses. I would no longer dwell on perceived unfairness or the inactions or others. I was not going to waste another second of my time or energy waiting for other people to mobilize me.

I realized waiting for external factors to create the perfect timing had trapped me into a stagnant life filled with flimsy excuses. I understood how my half-hearted attempts to create the life I knew I wanted, but didn't allow myself to have, had limited me and my ability to be happy. I didn't like feeling trapped, and I certainly didn't love my situation, so I actively decided to change it!

With fresh perspective, I set off on a magnificent world trip traveling through sixteen countries completely alone. It was, and remains, one of the most incredible experiences of my life and still positively impacts me today. I have grown in ways I could never have imagined, expanding myself not only mentally, but physically and spiritually. My personal and business skills have dramatically improved, and I've diversified myself. It took a lot of guts, but once I had done it, I was ecstatic! I had finally accomplished what I previously believed to be impossible.

Now, whenever I'm faced with a moment of doubt or uncertainty in situations that are challenging and seemingly impossible, I look back on my own life to seek out an exact moment of when I've solved a similar problem. There is nothing quite as powerful as building your confidence by using your own success story as your best example of what you can achieve.

It's fundamental to our human happiness to seek and strive for long-term fulfilment, even if finding it requires taking a leap of faith in yourself and venturing far beyond the boundaries of your natural comfort zone. The best part of all of this is knowing that finding your great life adventure is completely within your reach. It is always yours to control and steer in whichever direction you choose to take yourself.

Photo: Taking a scenic helicopter trip over the glaciers in Alaska.

Mike's phrase, *"do you know how much you are missing out on in life while waiting for other people?"* made me realize that developing excuses to hide behind was a way of building my own trap to prevent myself from finding genuine fulfilment. I was willing to blame my friends, girlfriend or others for not joining me on planned trips. I justified my decision not to travel by highlighting bad timing or questioning the safety level of a country. Of course, no one is suggesting you should act recklessly, but moving beyond problems and excuses allows the real solutions to present themselves naturally.

My former excuses inevitably only caused me frustration and anger, because I always felt like I was missing out. It made me complain and spread negative vibes, which only fueled the problems I was creating for myself. Ask yourself,

How satisfied am I with my personal life situation right now?

Photo: Swimming with elephants in the Mekong River, Laos.

Do you love your life, or are you willing to change it to create a happier, more fulfilling story? Use this page to explore some of the things you would like to change about your life as it is today.

Your life is in your own hands, and your hands only!

RULE 5

TAKE YOUR ADVICE FROM THE RIGHT PEOPLE

'The first condition of understanding a foreign country is to smell it.'

- RUDYARD KIPLING

Initially, thinking about where my travel advice was coming from didn't concern me much, but over time I have realized just how important it is to take advice from the right people. The type of advice you receive can change everything. It may be the crucial reason why you fail to achieve your goals. It could lead you down completely new and unimagined paths that are better than you had planned, and it can ultimately be the reason why you pack your bags to take that spectacular journey that will change your life forever.

If you want to become a billionaire, who should you take your advice from? Rich people of course! If poor people knew how to be rich, they wouldn't be poor, so they probably don't have the best advice about how to make a lot of money. Seek money advice from someone who has made millions, not from somebody who has read all about money but hasn't managed to make any.

The best advice comes from a place of true, first-hand understanding about how the situation works, and how it can be controlled to produce your desired outcome. This principal applies to just about everything but is especially relevant to travel advice. Travel is a subject where most people carry an opinion, even though many have never done much traveling themselves. Ask just about anyone for travel advice and you'll get something from them. Oftentimes, however, this kind of travel advice comes from people with no authentic travel experience, which can be more disruptive than it is helpful.

These amateur travel advisers can feel entitled to give advice on traveling and travel related topics. Sometimes, their advice is great and will catapult you to the next step, but sometimes this type of advice is based on their reading about travel rather than having genuine travel experience with tangible travel knowledge. Not all people can advise you truthfully with your best interests in mind, so travel advice from others often includes their own complex emotions and personal point of view regarding your travel plans. Before you take someone's travel advice to heart, it's worth running through a quick mental checklist in your head to give their advice credibility. Ask yourself:

→ Is this person giving me travel advice for financial gain, perhaps to sell a tour that earns commission or to recommend something they have a financial investment in?

→ Does the person advising me have any concern for how my travel plans might affect them personally?

→ Does this travel advice add value to my travel plans, and will it help me realize my own travel goals more easily?

This is usually most relevant with loved ones where strong emotions come into play. **Listening to your family and friends is great, but be careful not to confuse their unconditional love with valuable travel advice.** Family members, by default, feel obligated to share their opinions, but their input is not always going to be right for you.

A good example of this is between parents and their children, when a generational divide influences the accepted social or cultural behavior. Parents want to raise their children in the best conceivable way and can become trapped by their feelings of unconditional love. Ignorance, concern for their children's' safety, changes to social norms since they were young, and their fundamental duty to teach and advise their children how to survive can be particularly problematic, especially when parents allow their own lack of experience or differing points of view to stop their children from following their dreams.

This is not to say you should disrespect or discredit any of your close family members or potential travel advisers, but rather that you should filter your travel advice to align closely with your own travel ideals and personal growth story. Accept and listen to all the advice you receive, then run it all through your mental checklist to decide for yourself if you would like to follow it or ignore it.

Learning to think on your feet in the world of advice is a valuable tool. Let's take this story of 'Grandpa' as the gold standard for resolving family travel advice.

Grandpa has a great deal of experience when it comes to fishing. He's won all sorts of fishing tournaments in his small town in Michigan and has spent much of his life fishing on the Great Lakes. Grandpa can show you every trick on the lake to bring home the biggest fish, but he has never traveled outside of the state of Michigan or ventured beyond the confines of the life he knows. If becoming a fishing champion is your top goal, then there is no better person to ask than Grandpa, an experienced fisherman who knows everything there is to know about fishing.

If you would like to travel to Egypt, then you can be certain that Grandpa will be delighted to tell you everything he thinks he knows about Egypt, even though he doesn't know much about traveling there.

Being of a different generation, Grandpa is likely to discourage you from visiting Egypt out of fear for your safety, which in his view will be an expression of love and concern for you. To a person who only knows about Michigan, the Pyramids of Giza are an unfathomable destination in a far-off place that seems dangerous. He's likely thinking, "What if you get into trouble and can't get yourself out of it? How do the politics work, how safe is it, why is it so politically unstable?" Because Grandpa's only understanding of Egypt is what he has seen on the news, and the news by its very nature, is prone to reporting the dramas of a place rather than the magic, he is worried that visiting Egypt might be harmful. Of course, listening to Grandpa may be something you value, so giving him time to voice his opinion is a healthy step in creating a successful travel map and taking care of your relationship. Once you've heard his opinion, the next step is to address Grandpa's concerns with useful information and continue working on your own idea to visit Egypt.

STEP 1: DO YOUR RESEARCH, AND DO IT WELL

Read as much as possible about Egypt and try to answer every question you can think of. Find out what the currency is, learn about the politics and read up on any cultural requirements that you may need to adopt during your visit. Create an exit plan should things go wrong, then think of a creative way to help others feel happy about your plans. A great idea is to take Grandad to a local Egyptian cultural center in Michigan to show him the exciting side of why you wish to visit Egypt's Pyramids of Giza.

Next, research what you would most like to do during your time in Egypt. Find out how internal travel works, where to stay and where best to avoid. Draw up a strong plan that includes everything on your wish list in a way that works, is accessible, and safe. Visit travel blogs, explore your destination on social media, read news articles, and seek out lists of the absolute best experiences from reliable sources, trustworthy guidebooks and those first-hand advisors who have gone before you.

STEP 2: MAKE CONTACT WITH AT LEAST THREE PEOPLE WHO HAVE ALREADY BEEN THERE

As you build up your own personal database of information using educated travel advice, you'll start to collect the tips and tricks that other travelers have already discovered. Talk to your friends, message blog owners and follow inspiring travelers on social media. Leverage local knowledge and learn from their genuine first-hand insights. Draw from their network of connections around the world, ask for their restaurant recommendations, and discover which sights they enjoyed most. Then make a list of dos and don'ts to collate all the information into a clear plan that's easy to follow.

Share your research with others. Share it with those in your life who, like Grandpa, are anxious about your plans. This will help ease their concerns and encourage them to feel good about your travel dreams. Helping others understand your plans removes their doubt and sets you free from all those who may be holding you back or causing you to make excuses.

Step 3: Have confidence in yourself

Boost your confidence by connecting with people who are equally excited to travel and have a similar mindset as you. Join others on their travels or take part in a group tour if you feel more comfortable traveling with company. Follow the no excuse rules to shift your self-doubt and make the most of your travels.

Taking travel advice from the wrong places, such as Grandad's version of what travel to Egypt will look like, is one of the biggest reasons why travel goals can become severely set back or, in some cases, permanently shelved and never revisited. I've seen many friends and travel enthusiasts over the years who have appeared to have their travel plans firmly in place, but later lost confidence or failed to trust themselves with the advice they had taken. In the end, these people missed out on their big dreams and now live with regret for what they could so easily have done differently.

Making your own decisions and following your own beliefs is key to owning your success. Building a travel network to find the right people to get sound advice from takes time. It can seem challenging at first, but doing this builds momentum and fuels excitement! Trust the process. Remember that you will always encounter some resistance and criticism for doing the things you love, so take no heed and press on anyway. In the end, the rewards will be rich and plentiful.

Think about some of the people in your own life who may be holding you back when it comes to offering you their travel advice. **What might some of their fears be?**

What can you do to help ease their concerns and get them onboard with supporting your travel plans?

Photos: (Left) Meeting the llamas at Machu Picchu, Peru. (Right) Monks and monkeys at Angkor Wat, Siem Reap, Cambodia. (Bottom) Sipping cocktails in Cancun, Mexico.

Rule 6

Make Exponential Use of Your Time

'Time flies. It's up to you to be the navigator.'

- Robert Orben

Imagine it's a regular Friday afternoon when your boss comes over and says, "Why don't you take the next two weeks off work?" Would you stay at home wishing you had known sooner so you could have done something with the time, or would you just trust yourself, thank your luck, and take an unplanned adventure? This happened to me, and it turned out to be the trip of my dreams. Here's how it panned out in real time:

FRIDAY 5PM: I was given 2 weeks of unplanned, unexpected vacation time.

FRIDAY 6PM - 8PM: I freaked out, felt pumped and decided to go somewhere amazing. *But where in the world should I go?*

I identified my key parameters, which in this case was primarily a lack of time to prepare. I had a reasonably long amount of time off work to play with, which meant I could easily travel far and still get the most out of my chosen destination. Knowing this helped me focus my ideas on international destinations rather than domestic travel. Two other major constraints were visa restrictions and budget. I needed to travel to a country that didn't require me to apply for a visa, and I had a relatively low budget.

Using these clearly defined parameters, I knew I wanted to find a cheap, long-haul destination that either didn't require a visa or could process a visa on arrival.

Because I had already created my long-term travel vision and researched the places I most wanted to visit, I knew my money would go a long way in South-East Asia where the cost of living is generally quite low. By chance, my time off work happily coincided with the Asian shoulder season which also meant the flights were less full with great, cheap fares available. Accommodation was more affordable than it would have been in the peak season, so this made South-East Asia the perfect region.

I had been hoping to visit Cambodia for many years but had never really found the 'right time' to do it. Using this structured approach to travel planning showed me that the right time had conveniently found me. My positive attitude and can-do flexibility were ready to put my existing travel vision into action, so I made a quick decision to check off one of my top travel dreams with a last-minute trip to Angkor Wat in Siem Reap, Cambodia.

SATURDAY 8AM: Once I had picked where to go, all that remained was finalizing the logistics. I knew from my research that Cambodia would grant me a visa on arrival, and with a little further probing I found the cheapest point of entry was to fly through Thailand, where no visa was required for me as a German citizen. I booked a return flight to Bangkok, Thailand, and planned to take a public bus across the border into Cambodia.

Knowing accommodations in Cambodia were not running at full capacity gave me the flexibility to arrive with extraordinarily little lodging pre-booked. I would simply be able to arrive into Bangkok and create my itinerary as the trip progressed based on what I felt like doing each day. Within 48 hours, with close to zero preparation, I had mapped out a very loose sketch of what my time in Cambodia might look like, which happened to be the very first trip I had ever written into my travel vision.

How was it so easy to set these gears into motion? Simple. It's all about *using time wisely*. Everyone has twenty-four hours in a day, but some people seem to have more time than others.

Of course, we are all unique and all approach life differently, but even those who want and do the same things can end up with completely different results. **It's not about how much time we have. It's how we use our time that counts. How we allow different priorities to guide us creates the illusion that we have more, or less,**

time available. Some people focus on building a career, others on spending time with family or friends. Most people spend at least some of their time thinking "it would be so nice if I only had the time to... "

The truth about time is it doesn't matter how you choose to spend your time, if you spend it moving towards the direction of your dreams, as best you can, within your own parameters. Time and money work in similar ways, so much like the journey to financial freedom, in order to make the best use of time, it is first necessary to understand how you're using your time, so you can successfully structure your time to accommodate your top priorities.

As we move through the 9 No Excuse Travel Rules, it's becoming clear the common denominator in every rule is time. Time tracks how quickly and efficiently you get things done. The faster and more effective you are at realizing your goals and putting your travel vision into action, the more you can see and experience in your lifetime. Since there is a limited amount of time available, getting the most out of life is all about using time in the best possible way. **We cannot create time, but we can add value to the time that we do have.** The secret is to always prioritize efficiency, but *never* at the expense of opportunity. In other words, don't take shortcuts that sell you short, but *do* find the shortest path to the outcome you most want to achieve.

Like my spontaneous trip to Cambodia, the most important thing to remember when traveling is to always prioritize accepting opportunities over having the perfect plan. Once the window of opportunity closes, all planning becomes irrelevant.

In my situation, I would have missed out on the trip of a lifetime had I needed it to be the perfect trip or planned out every element of my itinerary in advance. By the time I had finished creating a full plan, I might not have had any time left to even go on a trip! I had dreamed of this vacation for a long time, but I had always saved it for the 'perfect time' not fully appreciating that the perfect time doesn't exist. This time spent in Cambodia became so much more than I could ever have expected, all because I saw my window of opportunity and blindly leapt through it into the adventure of a lifetime.

Oftentimes, opportunities are missed because we subconsciously don't think we'll have enough time to make the most of them. This is solved by learning to be more thoughtful and more resourceful when it comes to assigning time to your personal priorities.

Start by sharpening your priorities and deciding what's most important to you, then trimming away everything that detracts from what you would really like to be doing with your time. When you start to analyze how you are using your time, you'll start spotting trends in wasteful activities that can easily be removed to create more time for travel.

Take a moment to reflect on how easily your available time, or your perceived lack of time, affects your ability to travel. Think about how this relates to your travel vision, asking yourself:

What have I done today that brings me closer towards my travel goals?

What have I done today that's been wasteful of my time, or caused me to lose focus on my desire to travel?

You may like to take this a step further and track your actions daily until you have a clear picture of where your time is going, and where you can conserve time for more valuable activities. Keeping track of your time usage allows you to set a daily schedule to optimize your focus and bring you closer to realizing your goals.

Photo: Stunning scenery at Iguazu Falls, which lies neatly on the border between Argentina and Brazil in South America.

The ability to be flexible is a wonderful tool that can help you to think about your time differently. What if you were to take advantage of a long and seemingly 'inconvenient' wait in a boring place, such as the doctor's waiting room, and use the time to research top activities in your favorite destination?

If you take a train journey across Europe, why not study on the train? Next time you're sitting at a boarding gate waiting for a flight, grab your favorite book and read up on something you would love to know more about but never have the time to research. Chunks of time are everywhere, so anticipating these little pockets of free time, and making the most of them, sets you up for a path of continuous learning with seemingly endless travel opportunities always at your fingertips.

Thinking critically about small moments in life that can be used more efficiently, then implementing a high level of personal focus to use them, frees time and makes it easier to chase down the toughest goals. Time and focus multiply exponentially, which sends the value of every moment skyrocketing into a world of opportunity and success.

TIME ^{FOCUS} = THE VALUE OF A MOMENT

Creating a life filled with meaning is not about having time to spare, but about using available time to focus on things that matter, and drawing as much as possible from every possible opportunity that presents itself. As you learn to focus your attention on things that inspire you, you'll start to notice more windows of opportunity appearing in places you may never have thought to look.

Take the leap, one opportunity usually reveals another. This became so clear to me when I found an opportunity to live and work in America.

When I took up a contracted job in the automotive industry in California, I knew my time living in the States would be relatively short, but I saw it as an incredible window of opportunity to travel through the Americas. I also wanted to complete my Master's thesis in Financial Management so that I could head back to Germany well-prepared for the best jobs that would help me afford a life of travel.

There seemed to be too much on my plate. I was working in a busy, full-time job in Los Angeles where a myriad of adventures lay at my doorstep. I was also hoping to stay fit, keep up my gym routine, use the weekends to explore other states and maintain a vibrant social life. I had many critics who thought I would crash and burn, which only pushed me to find a way to juggle my goals even if it was difficult. I sat down and brainstormed the giant conundrum of how to get the most value out of my time living in California. Despite significant self-doubt, I came up with a plan.

I realized the only person stopping me from accomplishing my goals was me, so I shifted the focus away from feeling overwhelmed and sought out nuggets of time that could be used more efficiently. I started skipping our daily team lunch breaks to work on my thesis. I found a way to do my grocery shopping less frequently and switched weeknights on the beach for study time at home. I read academic papers during my Stairmaster or sauna sessions at the gym. On weekends, I studied in the car as we made our way to some of America's most magnificent national parks.

This relentless, intensive process required months of tremendous focus, discipline and effort. I used my time as wisely and as thoughtfully as I could, not wanting to waste a single hour of any day on things that could distract me from my goals. I was so determined to succeed that some people may have considered it to be a pure obsession, which it was.

Six months later, my dedication and determination rewarded me. I achieved all I had set out to accomplish. I completed my Master's Degree while living and working abroad. I traveled through much of America, kept up a healthy fitness regime and returned to Germany ready to win the kinds of jobs that now enable me to afford my life of travel today. I had created the life I wanted despite self-doubt or the opinions of so many people who believed it to be impossible. I focused on the possibility, and then I did it.

Photo: Forging strong business networks in Washington D.C.

There are moments when I look back and realize how focused I really was during those months in America, and it still amazes me how much is genuinely possible with a proper level of focus. Harnessing time effectively to unleash your true potential is a powerful tool that opens a plethora of opportunities. The best part is that anyone can do it, and everyone can learn to focus on what's really important to achieve their own personal and travel related goals.

When traveling the Americas, I hoped to take in as many travel experiences as possible in a relatively brief period of time. This was particularly constraining in Bolivia where long travel distances and inflated costs create unique parameters. I had a week available to see the whole country.

Staying focused, I asked myself what I really wanted to do during my seven days in Bolivia. My bucket list was longer than the week I had, so I designed a Bolivia travel vision that aimed to check off as much as possible during the limited time that I did have.

This is what I came up with for my Bolivian adventure:

✈ Mountain bike from La Paz to Coroico on the famous Death Road, the world's most dangerous road.

✈ Dance at a Bolivian party.

✈ Explore the historical city of La Paz.

✈ Hear the Pope speak to the Bolivians in La Paz.

✈ Trek through the Amazon Jungle.

✈ Visit Salar de Uyuni, the world's largest salt flats.

This seemed like a big task for a short week. I was tired, and Bolivia is so enormous that the best places easily justify taking a full week for each. I mapped out the events and distances. La Paz was relatively easy, but the rest of my travel vision posed some serious logistical challenges.

The Amazon was a flight away towards the eastern part of the country, while Salar de Uyuni National Park was located southwest on the Chilean border, also a flight away but in the complete opposite direction. The only possible way to make my itinerary happen was to go back and forth between destinations, so I tweaked my plan and reworked it into a more condensed itinerary.

I took the bus from Lake Titicaca, Peru, to ensure I arrived in La Paz on a Saturday morning. This worked perfectly for a late-night Bolivian dance party despite a ridiculously early 4:30am start for the next day's mountain bike tour. Little to no sleep did not drain my excitement to see the awesome scenery at the foot of the snow-covered Andes Mountains. At just over 15,000 feet, the power of adrenaline kicked in pretty quickly, and we set off on our mountain bikes to traverse 40 miles of winding mountain scenery from La Paz to Coroico, down the famous Death

Road[2]. The tour took several hours, required extreme caution and rewarded our courage with beautiful, seemingly endless mountain stretches that I will never forget.

The next day I woke up early to schedule a free city walking tour provided by the local students, and later snuck into the crowds to listen to the Pope's public address in the heart of La Paz. After a delicious Bolivian dinner, I spontaneously booked a 10-hour overnight bus trip to Salar de Uyuni, where I spent the next three days exploring the spectacular white salt flats and red lagoons in an out-of-this-world landscape.

Traveling through the night in both directions saved a night's accommodation and freed up an extra day for sightseeing, but the Amazon was still high on my wish list.

---

[2] IN 1995, DEATH ROAD BECAME RECOGNIZED AS THE WORLD'S MOST DANGEROUS ROAD. DURING THE HEIGHT OF ITS USE IT WAS ESTIMATED TO CLAIM AROUND 300 LIVES PER YEAR AS DRIVERS PLUNGED TO THEIR DEATHS INTO THE VALLEYS BELOW. IT'S NOW A JOY RIDE FOR TOURISTS, AND EASILY ONE OF THE WORLD'S MOST SCENIC MOUNTAIN BIKE RIDES. IT'S NOT FOR THE FEINT-HEARTED!

I made my way back to La Paz to grab my bags from the hotel before heading to the military airport to catch a cheaper, more time-flexible flight to the Amazon. Traveling to the Amazon in an older, but still reliable, military plane was a unique part of the adventure, and saved me both money and time.

Photo: Mountain biking down the famous Death Road, Bolivia.

My last three days in Bolivia rounded off a remarkable trip. I booked a group tour with people from all over the world who were just as excited about exploring the Amazon as I was. Being able to experience these amazing moments with new friends helped me realize once more just how valuable time can be when it is used in the right way. Being resourceful by staying focused on the things that are most important sets us free from our greatest limitations, allowing us to live with value, meaning and imagination. This trip was a dream!

Whenever you have moments of self-doubt, just take a minute to refocus your thoughts and craft a plan for the time and resources that you do have. Let your parameters work for you, then ignite your imagination and soar into your own adventure.

Whatever you do, make sure you're always ready to grab hold of every opportunity.

Take that leap to do the things you have always wanted to do. Do it now and do it wisely. Don't make the mistake of waiting for the perfect time to present itself. The perfect time doesn't exist, but your time can be used in a multitude of ways to really make the most out of every available minute.

When we use time wisely, life falls into place all by itself.

Rule 7
Show Up, No Matter What

*'Still round the corner there may wait a new road or a secret gate;
and though I oft have passed them by, a day will come at last when
I shall take the hidden paths that run west of the moon, east of the
sun.'*

- J.R.R. Tolkien

Visiting Cambodia exceeded my wildest expectations in every conceivable way because I showed up ready to make the most of every opportunity. **Each time you show up, you prevent the window of opportunity from closing shut before you have the chance to take it.**

Think of this another way. Opportunities seek out those who are willing to take them and give them meaning. If an opportunity passes you by, it's because you weren't willing to let it become what it wanted to be. Simply being there and being willing to allow opportunities to grow organically creates positive environments for opportunities to reach their full potential. I may have made my last-minute trip to Cambodia happen by harnessing a positive attitude, jumping at the opportunity to travel and using my time wisely, but this alone is not enough.

Successful travel means continuing to show up every day. By doing this, always saying yes and always being present in your own experiences, the window of opportunity is never allowed to close. Even though I had originally only planned to visit Angkor Wat, my trip quickly evolved into a series of life-changing travel experiences.

Rather than just passing through Bangkok airport as a logistical hop, I decided to stay a night to immerse myself in Thailand's legendary nightlife. I danced on the rooftops in vibrant bars, made fantastic friends, and set the tone for a fun-filled vacation in Cambodia.

My dream to see Angkor Wat temple complex was quickly fulfilled on arrival in Siem Reap, where something incredible happened. As I offered my donation to the temple's donation box, a praying monk looked up at me and smiled, so I returned the positivity and began talking with him. My commitment to showing up led to a friendly conversation, and I received a personal blessing from the monk who hoped to bring good luck and prosperity into my life. It was an unforgettable experience, forging a personal connection that many tourists miss out on. I could never have planned for this experience; it happened by chance.

Since I was already in the region, I decided to stretch my boundaries and visit neighboring countries, Vietnam and Laos. I delved deep into the culture, meeting up with strangers who later invited me to be part of the Lantern Festival during the full moon in the quaint city of Hoi An.

This was one of the calmest, most romantic moments I've enjoyed on my travels. It was beautiful and serene watching the lanterns float gently through the sky.

In Laos, I had the opportunity to swim with the elephants in the Mekong River in Luang Prabang, which was an amazing experience!

In the end, my trip to Asia, arranged on less than two days' notice, took me to four remarkably different countries. It exposed me to distinctly diverse cultures with a wealth of unique encounters that still shape me today. All of this was made possible because I showed up, opened myself to every opportunity and embraced a positive attitude to make the most of the limited time available to me.

Heading into the 'unknown' means different things to different people. Perhaps your unknown is a different part of the world that seems foreign yet appealing, or maybe it's the decision to follow an influential CEO into a world of entrepreneurship. As life changes, the unknown may become a new lifestyle filled with kids and relationships, or newfound freedom to live your life the way you've always dreamed at the end of an unhappy marriage.

Nearly always, arising opportunities will take you towards the unknown, which is a good thing.

Photo: Breakfast with an amazing view in Hong Kong.

Showing up lets you take advantage of every arising opportunity. Being present, both physically and mentally, allows you to get in touch with the unknown places in your life to feel more open to everything this amazing world has to offer.

You might attend a charity event in a different city and get to know some highly successful connections who can launch your career into a new direction, or you may travel to Brazil for a few vacation days only to meet the love of your life on the beach. Perhaps you'll fall in love with the Italian culture at the foot of Rome's magnificent Colosseum, where you'll find yourself inspired to finally learn Italian, or maybe you'll discover you're more suited to a slower, softer pace in South-East Asia. The possibilities in travel are truly endless.

Each one of your travel-related activities is likely to squeeze you out of your comfort zone, flinging you into an unknown environment that's simply oozing with new possibilities and unclaimed opportunities. Your job is to test the waters to figure out what floats your heart. To do this, you need to show up and be willing to try new things. You need to take initiative and explore things that may at first seem strange to you. This builds your resilience against all the things that hold you back.

By showing up every day you'll refine your ability to seek out and take advantage of unexpected opportunities across all aspects of your life. You may find the network you built in India later becomes the cornerstone of your successful fashion company in America, or perhaps a boring seminar you didn't think you had time to attend will change the course of your career for the best. Opportunity is always there for the taking if you are willing to open yourself up to finding it.

A big part of having the ability to always show up is recognizing how feelings of exhaustion can, at times, make it extremely difficult to make the effort; there are moments when we all want to slow down and relax, and these days are important too.

Looking after yourself means taking time to unwind when needed, but there is a difference between relaxing and not doing anything. When you are not using your time to unwind, but are instead just wasting time doing nothing, you can be assured that someone else is out there taking the opportunities you are missing out on.

Every time you fail to show up, somebody else will take your place, allowing the opportunity to pass you by and fall into someone else's good fortune. No goals are easily reached by being complacent, and nobody has ever become a traveling globetrotter by sitting on the sofa. Authentic travel requires passion, discipline, and commitment, which starts with the simple act of taking initiative and making the effort to always show up ready to shine.

History, culture, nature, relaxation, food, and so many more unknown experiences are just some of the treats that await you when you start seeking out opportunities and running head-first into every adventure you find.

EXERCISE

Gather pictures of the kinds of opportunities you would like to show up for. Keep them together in a box or a journal, then whenever you're feeling tired or demotivated, spend a few minutes looking through your box of dreams and choose one for your next adventure.

Photo: Diving with sharks in the Bahamas!

My travels have profoundly changed my life by opening me up to new ways of thinking. I've learned to always say yes first, then iron the details out later. Many of my travel adventures have been the happy, unexpected result of being in the right place at the right time. I would like to share some of the highlights of these situations with you. I hope you'll feel inspired to discover your own adventures in the endless sea of opportunity that is around all of us, all the time.

Camping with Brown Bears in Yosemite, California

In my opinion the USA is one of the world's most beautiful, diverse countries. Hiking through each of the national parks in several different states has given me a deep appreciation for nature and the gorgeous beauty of the earth. When I was living in Long Beach, my circle of friends frequently planned trips to California's top national parks, so I got to explore the magnificent and widely praised Yosemite National Park. We had three days to hike in these beautiful mountains, which was challenging, but I used my time and energy wisely. It was magical watching the stars from our campsite in such a pure, remote setting so far removed from the bright city lights. The highlight of course was seeing brown bears in their natural habitat!

HAVING DINNER WITH A COMMISSIONER OF THE EUROPEAN PARLIAMENT IN BRUSSELS

For a short while, I lived in Luxembourg where I supported the Merger & Acquisition projects for a major supplier to the automotive industry. By carefully nurturing my business relationships, persistently developing rapport through email exchanges and swapping old family stories, I whittled out an opportunity to drive to Brussels for dinner with a commissioner of the European Parliament. We enjoyed an extremely interesting exchange of views that has not only widened my business network but expanded my thinking into multiple new directions.

Gliding through the Austrian alps to Venice, Just to Drink Italian Espresso!

My sister's landlord in Austria was a dedicated pilot flying all sorts of gliders and small planes. I was living in Detroit at that time and knew an upcoming business trip to Germany had a very tight schedule with little time for extra activities. An introduction to the Austrian landlord gave me an easy opportunity to visit Italy, so after my business trip, I drove five hours from Germany to Austria for a glide flight. We soared across the magnificent Austrian Alps into Venice, where we stopped for an authentic Italian coffee on the banks of the Grand Canal.

Admiring Jerusalem from the Mount of Olives

Israel is worthy of an extended trip but doesn't need to take a long time to really get the best out of it. While working in Germany, a few of us decided to take a last-minute, $100 long weekend break to Tel Aviv. In just three days, we experienced a whirlwind tour of Jerusalem and Bethlehem, then floated gracefully on the surface of the Dead Sea. The highlight was standing where Jesus stood on the Mount of Olives, admiring the Old City of Jerusalem, stretched out below me as far the eye can see. It was completely mesmerizing!

PARTYING WITH HUGH HEFNER AT THE PLAYBOY MANSION

I had never really heard of a situation that would allow me, an ordinary guy from Germany, to attend one of the famous Playboy mansion parties in Los Angeles. It seemed absurd, until I met the right crowd of friends during my semester studying abroad at San Diego State University. I built a network of friends who told me about some crazy parties at the Playboy mansion. Eventually, I received a secret, coveted invite. It was an unbelievable event that I will never forget, made special by the personal invitation received through a well-earned connection. I even got to meet Hugh Hefner!

ATTENDING A PERUVIAN WEDDING WITH OVER 500 PEOPLE!

A Peruvian wedding is something to behold, so when I received an invitation to celebrate the wedding of one of my best friends in the gorgeous city of Lima, I simply couldn't turn it down. Work was extremely busy, but I managed to take a four-day weekend to attend and booked an extremely tight schedule to Peru. It seemed crazy to almost everyone I talked to, but it was so worth the effort. Over 500 people attended the wedding, and the opportunity to be part of such a special event was a rare treat. To top off the trip, I managed to squeeze in a fun sandboarding adventure in the oasis of Peru's Bellastas islands.

HIKING IN THE SAHARA DESERT

Teaming up with a dedicated travel buddy for a $70 round trip from Frankfurt to Marrakech, Morocco, was an enticing idea. Our plan was to hike in the Sahara Desert as a group of four, but when two of our friends cancelled on short notice due to political instability in surrounding countries, we decided to abandon our original plan and took a jeep to the Sahara, where we enjoyed our hike without them. This was one of my favorite, most exhilarating trips, made even more exciting by the knowledge that we very nearly didn't do it!

EXPLORING THE INNER CHAMBERS OF THE PYRAMIDS OF GIZA

While I was in Jordan visiting Petra, one of the ancient Wonders of the World, I met up with a friend who put me in contact with an archeology professor. The professor was authorized to take visitors into the interior chambers of the Pyramids of Giza at around the same time I had planned to visit Egypt with another friend from Florida.

By being in the right place at the right time, I was able to combine my planned tour of Egypt with the professor's expedition into the pyramid, letting me experience two world wonders within the same adventure; the Pyramids of Giza and the Lighthouse of Alexandria. Through successful networking, I experienced a unique perspective of the Pyramids of Giza. I was able to travel off-the-beaten track, deep into the chambers of these ancient structures in a way that is more personal and interesting than most travelers are able to experience it.

MEETING A WONDERFUL GIRL IN A HAMMAN BATH, ISTANBUL

Istanbul is a delight for the senses! Half the city is in Asia, and the other half in Europe, so it's a real melting pot of history and culture. I was visiting Istanbul with a few friends to celebrate New Year's Eve, and my hotel had a relaxing Hamman spa bath on the premises. The real surprise of this trip was to meet an amazing girl from Romania in our hotel spa. Bumping into her during a Hamman bath session in the heart of Istanbul was strangely captivating, and she became my girlfriend, highlighting how life sometimes takes its own course when we show up at the right time and place for an unexpected adventure. I was extremely impressed by her ability to speak nine different languages. She loved

Germany and spoke German fluently despite having never lived there herself. Being open to possibilities let a wonderful new person into my life. I was hooked!

DINNER WITH STRANGERS IN ECUADOR & ARMENIA

During my flight back from the Galapagos Islands I chatted with a wonderful, friendly woman from Quito. We developed such easy rapport that when we arrived in Quito, she extended an invitation for me to have dinner with her whole family at a 5-star restaurant. What an amazing show of genuine, warm hospitality enjoyed over a delicious local meal. These friends will always be welcome in my home because of this chance encounter.

A similar experience happened during our Jeep tour through Georgia, Azerbaijan and Armenia. While crossing the border from Georgia into Armenia by car, my friend Gerald and I had to purchase car insurance. During this process, four Armenian soldiers invited us to share their supper. They generously gave us their bread, tomatoes, cheese and local specialties. It was a real pleasure to have dinner with them. Their final gesture was to bid us farewell with a respectful salute. I will never forget their warm invite, and the interesting conversations we enjoyed together at the border.

HELPING OTHERS AROUND THE WORLD

Helping other people in any way possible is one of the most fulfilling things you can do on your travels. Frankly, I never really understood this when I was younger, but as time and experience have molded me into a more rounded person, I now find immense pleasure in helping others wherever possible.

Whether you donate your time, money or energy to helping others, your support is far more rewarding than you'll ever imagine. In many cases, these efforts will exponentially multiply the positive effects felt by those you support, which is richly rewarding for everyone. Traveling the world will enlarge your emotional spectrum and global understanding to hopefully inspire you to help whomever you can, whenever you can, more often, even if you already have a predisposition for helping others.

Your presence alone has a unique impact on the communities you'll encounter. Remember, each time you show up at a charity event or offer to volunteer, you can, and likely will, change someone's life forever.

Showing up isn't always easy and may not always work out in your favor, but by showing up, you are giving yourself the best chance to take every opportunity that comes your way. Not showing up guarantees you to miss out.

Whenever you feel like giving up because you are not immediately seeing the benefit of your efforts, just remember that showing up will always teach you something you can use in the future. If you can stick with it, and always show up, regardless of any obstacles you face, you will open yourself to a world you may never have otherwise imagined. Being open creates genuine, authentic happiness in the life you have always dreamed of.

Photo: Taking in the dramatic scenery in Monument Valley, one of America's most iconic national parks.

Rule 8

Tap Into Your Travel Creativity

'The important thing is not to stop questioning. Curiosity has its own reason for existing.'

- Albert Einstein

We explored in the previous chapter how showing up is essential if you wish to fully take part in life, but simply showing up will not always get you where you want to be. Sometimes more is needed, so once you've shown up and chosen the opportunities you like best, the next step is to get rid of any roadblocks that may be standing between you and your end goal. This is particularly true when it comes to chasing travel opportunities, because, when it comes to travel, things are often not as linear as they may seem.

This is where having a passionate sense of travel creativity really comes into play. Travel creativity is a tool to master and overcome travel-related challenges as they arise, the art of thinking on your feet and not getting bogged down by unexpected mishaps. Having great travel creativity requires the ability to be resourceful, and to solve problems using lateral thinking.

Photo: Soaring over the Austrian Alps in a glider plane.

The best part about travel problems is they usually take you down a path you otherwise may not have considered, and more often than not, the new road presents a better overall experience than the original plan. Most seasoned travelers don't find their travel adventures by simply following their initial travel game plan. Multiple obstacles are inevitable, so the more adept you are at thinking creatively to navigate yourself through unexpected situations, the more rewarding your travel experience will be.

Unpredictable incidents will force you to rethink or adjust your ideas, sometimes drastically. Prepare for the likelihood of this in advance, then go with the flow and just allow the journey of travel to guide you through whatever challenge you may be faced with. From a personal point of view, traveling the world on my own has been the biggest factor in helping me develop my sense of travel creativity. Letting go of the need to rely on others has empowered me to genuinely resolve any kind of surprise drama, which has in turn caused me to seek out the unexpected and less-explored parts of the world for greater rewards.

I now travel with far less planning than I started out with, with a higher level of creative thinking every step of the way. I take every day as it comes, trusting that no problem is ever going to be too big to be solved. Nourishing my travel creativity spills into every aspect of my life, developing a keen sense of resilience that's equally useful in all kinds of scenarios from work to relationships and everything in-between. Travel skills are strong, transferrable skills that help us live better every day.

Consider the story of the two hungry sisters and their clever grandmother:

> *'Grandma Barbara left some lemons in the kitchen and asked her two hungry granddaughters, Lisa and Sarah, to find a way to share the odd number of lemons appropriately.*
>
> *Before Grandma Barbara left, she encouraged her granddaughters to use creative thinking to make a wise decision on how to make best use of*

the lemons. The lemons could not be divided equally, so they could either split the lemons in such a way that one sister won more than her fair share or find a way to compromise.

After much discussion, the sisters finally questioned their individual needs and realized that each sister had completely different goals. Lisa was looking for the inner part of the lemons to make some fresh lemonade, while Sarah was only interested in the rind to bake her favorite lemon zest cake. By communicating their needs and looking at the lemons from a different perspective, both sisters were able to share the lemons according to their individual wishes without wasting any of the lemons.

Despite starting out with limited resources, the development of their creative thinking meant they were able to generate a workable solution that gave both sisters exactly what they were looking for.'

Most people focus on their own goals first, however, when we learn to see the full picture and account for the needs of others, we bring fresh ideas to just about any challenge. **By seeking to understand the interests and goals of others, we better stimulate our own creative thinking.** Your travels may at times give you lemons, but the best outcome is not always to make lemonade. You may just find lemon zest cake is a sweeter, tastier treat!

Every journey I've been on has required some degree of travel creativity, which has forced me to adapt myself to evolving situations. Entering unfamiliar territories around the world has provided the perfect playground to nurture my travel creativity, which has further enhanced my personal development in all aspects of living a happier, more fulfilling life.

A Logistical Conundrum in Cape Town, South Africa

It was a hot summer's day in South Africa. I was sitting in the back of a cab on the way to Cape Town airport when I realized the last remnants of my cash in the local currency wasn't enough to pay for my ride. When we arrived at the airport, I asked to pay with a credit card, but unfortunately the driver couldn't accept cards, leaving me unable to pay. I asked him to wait while I took a quick trip to the ATM, but this too declined my card, so the cab driver called the police to argue his missing fare.

With the arrival of the police imminent, I tried to check in for my flight to Sydney only to find the airline check-in attendant was unable to match my Australian visa to my current passport. To top it all, my phone battery had gone flat, so in addition to not being able to access money to pay for my cab ride or check in for my flight, I was also unable to open my emails to get the correct visa number as sent to me by the Australian Embassy. Precious time was being wasted, and I risked missing my flight.

Thinking on my feet, I found a way to resolve all the issues simultaneously. I asked the airline's check-in attendant to charge my phone, which she thankfully agreed to do, then coordinated with the cab driver to figure out a way to pay for my cab ride. I offered to fill his car with gas in exchange for the lift to the airport and was luckily able to pay with a credit card at the gas station. This also meant my payment totaled more than the cab fare to make up for the inconvenience I had caused the driver.

The cab driver was extremely happy to receive a full tank of gas, so he returned me to the airport where I was able to turn on my fully charged phone to access my emails. This resolved the issue with my visa, so I was finally able to check in for my flight.

Assessing the totality of my challenges, asking for help and being open to the needs of others gave me the right mental tools to solve all of my problems using creative thinking. The check-in attendant wanted to see proof of my paperwork, the cab driver needed resources to run his business, and I needed a fully charged phone. We all needed the police to be gone, so between us we worked together to find a solution that solved everyone's problem simultaneously.

There is always a solution, but challenges should be identified and creatively resolved rather than simply running for the obvious answer that may not always be the right route forward.

SWEET TALKING MY WAY INTO A FANCY WORLD CLASS RESTAURANT IN LIMA, PERU

Being rather charming, I promised my girlfriend at the time an amazing dinner at one of the top restaurants in Lima, not realizing the waiting time for a sought-after restaurant is several months, not an hour or two. I showed up anyway and decided to sweet talk my way in by chatting to the management team. I told them I was an international traveler and Peruvian food lover on a limited schedule, then explained how I was desperately trying to impress my date who I had already told the table was booked. I also offered a personal gift as a warm gesture in exchange for any chance of being able to deliver on my promises.

My kindness was rewarded; the manager did everything he could to help me out of the pickle I had caused for myself. He found us two seats at the bar in the lower area of the restaurant, where we enjoyed cocktails and appetizers before heading up to our romantic table on the top floor. Luckily, everything worked out well, and the date was a success. She never did find out about our 'up in the air' last-minute perfect date plans![3]

ICE CREAM HOPPING IN OAHU, HAWAII

I was preparing to move back to Germany from San Diego when we decided to squeeze in a last-minute trip to the gorgeous island of Oahu, Hawaii. We arranged to spend

---

[3] I'M GUESSING SHE MIGHT KNOW ABOUT IT NOW, THOUGH.

a week on Oahu and mapped out a tight but adventurous itinerary. One of our goals was to spend a day beach hopping down every beach on the island, but it wasn't long before we reached the end of the local bus timetable and found ourselves stranded at a random beach in the middle of nowhere.

Wondering what to do, we headed to a nearby ice cream truck to assess the situation over tasty refreshments. We started chatting to the driver. He too was a beach hopper and planned to make his way along the coast to the very same beaches we wished to visit, selling ice cream to the sunbathing tourists. It was a perfect solution to our problem, and our friendly rapport made it easy to convince him to take us along for the ride. Hopping on and off an ice cream truck was an innovative way to visit all the beaches while having fun meeting new people.

Some may argue that a rental car would have allowed us more flexibility, but this incident taught us how kindness and creative thinking can go a long way in making new friends. We created a unique travel experience in a beautiful place and learned a lot about ice cream!

Road Tripping Without a Car in Alaska

After visiting a real estate convention in Las Vegas, I was eager to extend my stay with a short trip up to Anchorage and Seward in Alaska. I was excited, and thought I was extremely well-prepared, but unfortunately, when I tried to collect my rental car at Anchorage Airport I realized that my American driver's license had expired 6 days earlier. I was not legally allowed to drive in the USA, which is the main part of a successful road trip!

Alaska is an expansive destination, so I took stock of my options and realized being flexible was the only way the trip could happen as planned. I chatted to a friendly cab driver named Kim, from Seoul, which was an ideal starting point for my first mini trip to Seward. Kim not only cut me a fair deal, but also turned out to be an awesome tour guide who was willing to go above and beyond to show me some of Alaska's stunning scenery. We stopped for moose sightings, viewed spectacular glaciers and discussed Kim's top tour recommendations for my time in Seward.

Once in Seward I mostly walked, found rides with local tour guides and hotel managers or made appropriate use of Seward's only Uber driver to check all the boxes on my original itinerary. Luckily, I had also arranged my trip through a brilliant travel agent who was able to readjust my plans as needed, which in this case was very welcome. My challenging situation was caused entirely by my own lack of preparation, which meant that I needed to be more flexible and more reliant on others than I would otherwise have liked to have been, but this flexibility is also what opened me up to experiences I may not have discovered in Alaska.

On my way back from Seward to Anchorage, I took the scenic train, which is easily one of the world's most amazing rail journeys, but not something I would naturally have included in a road trip itinerary. It was beautiful and worth every minute!

Photo: Fishing for salmon in Seward, Alaska.

EXERCISE

Think of a time when you have creatively gotten yourself out of a tricky situation. How did you do it, and what did you learn from it?

One of the easiest ways to develop creative thinking in travel is to make smart use of flight layovers. Oftentimes, direct flights to sought after destinations, such as the Greek Islands, can be expensive, whereas less favorable flights with overnight layovers can often be far cheaper and a lot more interesting. I've always considered layovers to be a positive part of travel. They facilitate extra time to have fun in an unexplored destination that you may otherwise not have visited.

Booking a cheap round trip flight to Athens, including an overnight stay at a luxurious hotel in Paris, can cost about the same as a direct flight to Santorini and comes with the added joy of a ferry ride from Athens to Santorini.

You can mix this up even further by booking your flight home through a different city, as we did some years ago when we visited the beautiful island of Santorini with bookend city breaks in both Paris and Rome. Seeing these amazing cities on either side of our Greek Island vacation meant our trip to Greece was not only more affordable, but also included two bonus mini vacations.

The more you practice your travel creativity, the more you'll be able to weather the storms and solve problems as and when they arise.

Developing your travel creativity is the ideal way to enhance and spice up your travel experiences, encouraging you to create new plans on the fly and changing anything you don't love about your current adventure so it better aligns with your travel vision. There is absolutely nothing wrong with changing your ideas as your travel itinerary progresses. If you don't love it, change it!

Break some rules and train yourself how to think about things differently. Be open, kind and flexible to people and situations that can stimulate your creative thinking skills.

The trips that don't go according to your plans are usually the most memorable and rewarding, so nurturing this approach to creative travel fosters spontaneity that inspires you to explore new surroundings. This, in turn, will further enhance your travel creativity. Start planning your next trip right now, then mobilize your travel creativity to make it remarkable. I would be delighted to hear about your personal travel stories and how you have used your own travel creativity, so feel free to reach out and tell me all about it at any time!

Photo: Picturesque scenery at Neuschwanstein Castle in Germany.

Rule 9

Take Decisive Travel Action

'A ship in harbor is safe, but that's not why ships were built.'

- John A. Shedd

Taking decisive travel action is the most important rule in the book, because this is the step that ultimately determines whether you reach your travel goals or let them become your latest unfinished project. Action is the cornerstone of everything, the underlying thread that holds all the No Excuse Travel Rules together. Taking decisive action is what makes your travel dreams a reality.

As I made my way across the globe exploring so many incredible destinations, cultures, lifestyles, historical relics and world wonders, I discovered there are three fundamental groups of people. Each group embraces a different type of mentality, which has a profound impact on the person's own actions and influences the others within their travel network.

THE BLAMERS AND COMPLAINERS

"My friends have let me down, so now my trip is cancelled."

This group will always find something that makes them feel dissatisfied with their current situation. Their mood and attitude prevent them from doing things they want to do, preferring instead to wait around for others, then always feeling disappointed when they miss out on the good times.

Blamers and complainers tend to rely on others to mobilize their actions, rather than just doing things for themselves. This gives them a reason to complain about those who let them down, which only fuels the cycle of blaming, and complaining. Unfavorable circumstances such as work, relationships, lack of time, lack of money, and lack of travel companions make easy excuses, so persistent complainers who blame others for their failures never fully reach their travel goals.

THE PROCRASTINATORS

"I would love to travel, but
perhaps it will be better saved for another time."

These kinds of travelers recognize travel is within their reach, and do take responsibility for their inaction, but somehow always fail to get started.

The procrastinators are always waiting for the stars to align so that their dream plan can fall into place automatically, but, the 'perfect time' doesn't exist so they're always left waiting for tomorrow.

Procrastinators dream big and aren't afraid to employ vivid imagination to visualize their travel goals, but they're afraid to dive deep and let go of their perceived stability. As life passes them by, the procrastinators worry about insecurity, obscurity, other people's opinions, fear of the unknown and their self-imposed requirement of finding the 'perfect time' to start.

THE BELIEVERS & THE DOERS

"I want to travel, so that's what I'll do!"

The believers and the doers are brave travelers who take their ideas and rally them into action. They're not afraid to chase their dreams, knowing that if they wait around for the perfect time, they will never get off the ground.

These are the people who understand what they want in life, and take matters into their own hands to do what they need to do to reach their goals. They're not afraid of failure because they know there's no such thing as failure. Their powerful flexibility and creative problem-solving skills turn their challenges into opportunities in a perpetual state of motion and growth.

These people aren't always popular, but they're happy. Blamers and complainers find believers and doers frustrating, believing the doers to be responsible for their own inaction. Procrastinators wonder how the doers do it, looking to doers with a sense of bewilderment that oftentimes only fuels their own tendencies to find the right time so that they too, can do things.

The doers believe in all the possibilities that lie in endless opportunities, so they make no time to blame others or complain about their situation. They understand procrastination will only hold them back, so they set out and do all the things they would like to do on their own terms.

This relentless positive attitude to always execute ideas creates the kind of travel behaviors that encourage doers to venture further out, reaching far beyond their natural comfort zones in search of bigger, more daring ideas. Their travel actions determine their travel success, and they revel in taking responsibility for their own travel vision. The more they travel, the more they dream and the more they achieve. Believers and doers are willing to put the time, energy and work required to get their adventures into action and make their own travel dreams their own reality.

Phot: Walking with lions in Zimbabwe, Africa.

When I turned thirty and looked back on my life, I realized I've travelled to over eighty countries and have lived and worked around the world. I've lived in big cities and small communities, building a solid network of global friends and diverse business contacts. I've reached my dream of seeing all the remaining Ancient and New Wonders of the World, shared my story with others in the hope that they too will feel inspired to travel, and set up a stable stream of income to fund my life of travel. I've achieved everything I set out to do.

Most importantly, I realized that I'm happy, and learned that anyone and everyone can be happy if they embrace the right kind of attitude.

Happiness has a simple formula. Decide on the amazing things you want to do with your life, work out your parameters, use your creative thinking to resolve your challenges, stop making excuses, believe you can have all the things you want out of life, then head out into the world to do them.

There is always a way, if you want there to be.

How do you see yourself - are you a blamer and complainer, a procrastinator or a believer and a doer?

Why do you see yourself this way and how can you take more action to do more?

Photo: Visiting Petra, one of the 7 New Wonders of the World, in Jordan.

Bringing It All Together

Travel opportunities open us up, encouraging us to extract more out of every moment of our lives, if we're willing to show up and make the most of everything that comes our way. The same approach applies to business ventures, family life, career development and personal projects. It infuses success into every area of our personal and emotional wellbeing.

If you want something, and are willing to take it, it is fully and completely within your control to go out and get it.

Becoming a world traveler is easy, and within the reach of everybody, no matter how big or small your travel plans are, how your budget looks, or what kind of socio-economic background you come from. The key is to stay disciplined, and follow the No Excuse Travel Rules until you reach your goals.

Polish your travel dreams to create a vision you know you would like to achieve. Understand what it is that you want to do, so you can give yourself the right tools to achieve it, then make a commitment to yourself to allow yourself to experience everything your vision entails.

Be grateful for the opportunities you have and leverage your sense of purpose to think positively, breathing an open-minded attitude into everything you do. If you don't love something about your current situation, change it or do it differently, until you love everything about your life.

You, and only you, are responsible for the experiences you create for yourself.

Learn from those who have gone before you, always take your advice from trustworthy sources, and filter out anyone who comes between you and your dreams. Use every moment you have wisely. Make exponential use of your time to pull as much as possible from every pocket of free time that comes your way.

Own your travel plan. Always be ready to jump into possibility and opportunity with both feet. Tap into your creative mindset to think differently when things don't go your way. Nurture your ability to see things with new perspective and continuously write new adventures for yourself.

Then act. Act on your plans, act on your ideas, act on every positive thought you have until travel becomes your way of life, and the traveling mindset becomes second nature to you. Don't wait for the perfect time, do it now. Do it with heart, and most of all, do it for yourself. The bigger the action, the better the experience and the more likely you'll expand yourself into new, dynamic journeys that you may never have thought possible.

Take responsibility for your life, and make a conscious decision to travel on your own terms. Ignore the negativity and naysayers around you. Keep yourself on track and visualize your dreams. Discipline, consistency, persistence and massive travel actions will compound over time to unleash your greatest potential, opening your life up to all the travel that you have always dreamed of. So, don't fall into the trap of being a blamer or complainer, stop procrastinating and join the believers and the doers who make bold decisions to live full, adventurous lives!

Make no excuses, so you can live with no regrets!

The world is yours; I'll see you there!
Philipp Gloeckl

Photos: (Top) Living in Los Angeles, USA.

(Bottom) Walking on the Great Wall of China in Beijing, China.

Photo: Soaking up the serene beauty at the Taj Mahal, India.

SHARE YOUR ADVENTURE

Now that you have all the steps for Making Your Travel Dreams a Reality at your fingertips, I encourage you to leave a review and inspire others to start their world-travel journey!

To explore the TravelPeeGee Experience in more depth, please visit **www.travelpeegee.com.**

For questions, suggestions, or media inquiries, please, send me an email to **info@travelpeegee.com**

Made in the USA
Monee, IL
22 December 2020